MW01173892

IF THIS CHALKBOARD COULD TALK

STORIES FROM GLOBAL EDUCATORS TO MAKE YOU LAUGH, CRY, SHAKE YOUR HEAD AND SAY...
YOU CAN'T MAKE THIS UP

VOLUME 1

PRODUCTION

If This Chalkboard Could Talk
By Dr. Matthew X. Joseph
Volume 1
Copyright © 2023

https://xfactoredu.org

X-Factor EDU

Our Mission Statement:

Be Unapologetically
YOU

Thank you to all our X-Factor partners!
Your efforts will directly support educators' growth and access to resources necessary for improving teaching and learning. Because of you, we are all Stronger Together.

Proud to support #SameHere Schools programs. 100% profits from "If This Chalkboard Could Talk" will go toward supporting schools bring in #SameHere to support students and a positive culture.

All contributors and X-Factor EDU donated their time and intellectual property to ensure we continue to support our schools and to ensure we continue to laugh and find joy in our work.

#SameHere

THE GLOBAL MENTAL HEALTH MOVEMENT

#SameHere Schools programs support students' social and emotional development, and their sense of connection to the teachers, staff, and their peers. The #SameHereSchools program creates a cultural shift within schools, providing a safe atmosphere for students to express themselves openly and communicate when they are dealing with emotional or mental health challenges – whether they be originating at home, in school, or out in the community

The #SameHereSchools program creates a cultural shift within schools, providing a safe atmosphere for students to express themselves openly and communicate when they are dealing with emotional or mental health challenges – whether they be originating at home, in school, or out in the community.

Learn more at www.xfactoredu.org/samehere

Table of Contents

FOREWORD

By Marialice B.F.X. Curran, Ph.D.

Growing up, my family lived in my parents' starter home. Over 25 years later, they moved on to their next home. I can't use the word "retirement" home because my mom never used that word. Instead, she always said it was their "next chapter" home which happened to be located on a corner lot. The dictionary defines a corner as a place where two or more sides meet and for my parents, this new home was, literally and figuratively, A Turn in the Road for them. As I write this now, I find myself in my own Turn in the Road, and perhaps you feel the same way.

Maybe it's because the pandemic turned our world upside down. Since February 27, 2020, when schools shut down, sporting events were canceled, and we collectively experienced school, play, and work over Zoom, it has felt like we've been living in a really bad sci-fi movie. In fact, it feels like two completely different worlds: time before (the pandemic) and time now.

In the novel *Cat's Eye,* Margret Atwood captures how I've always viewed time:

Time is not a line but a dimension, like the dimensions of space. If you can bend space, you can bend time also, and if you knew enough and could move faster than light, you could travel backward in time and exist in two places at once...But I began then to think of time as having a shape, something you could see, like a series of liquid transparencies, one laid on top of another. You don't look back a long time but down through it, like water. Sometimes this comes to the surface, sometimes that, sometimes nothing. Nothing goes away.

How many of us have had things come to the surface, especially these past three years? I imagine this has happened to each of us, no matter how young or old you are, where you live, what language(s) you speak, or which traditions and cultures you practice. What we have collectively endured is a reminder to us all that we are one world, one human race, and most importantly, that we need each other.

In May 2020, I was fortunate enough to meet Eric Kussin, the founder of #SameHereGlobal during Mental Health Awareness Month. During that first interaction, I learned about how #SameHereGlobal is changing the narrative around mental health. We've all been conditioned to think about mental health as us-versus-them, a 1-in-5 issue where some either have "it" with a label (insert depression, anxiety, PTSD, etc.) or they don't.

The #SameHereGlobal mission embraces an inclusive 5-in-5 approach and further validates the idea that we all experience challenges and struggles in life. Their American Sign Language (ASL) inspired logo also reinforces this inclusive message with a brightly colored hand signing "same" as a reminder that there are more things that connect us than divide us.

Eric has become a lifeline for me and the ultimate connector to mental health resources, both personally and professionally. Despite the worst parts of this pandemic, Eric and his #SameHereSchools programs bring important conversations to school communities around the world in order for us to prioritize mental health at school, home, play, and work.

Just like the Atwood quote, we all experience moments when things come to the surface. Over time, I've learned that we need the 5-in-5 #SameHereGlobal message in local, global, and digital communities. This message helps us create more opportunities to see and value the human sitting next to us, around the world, and across the screen. We need to experience what connects us, what makes us human:

- If you have experienced isolation and loneliness during the pandemic, same here.
- If you have lost loved ones during the pandemic, same here.
- If you have felt out of control during the pandemic, same here.
- If you have endured a sense of betrayal during the pandemic, same here.
- If you have loved someone who has died by suicide, same here.

This list could go on and on, but the important thing to note is when we share our #SameHereGlobal stories, we not only change the narrative around mental health, but we also feel seen, we feel heard, we feel understood, and we feel a part of something bigger than ourselves.

Personally, a lot has come to the surface for me, and that's the reason why I asked if I could write the foreword to this book. In doing so, I find myself a different person than I was before the start of the pandemic. My circle is smaller, my focus and passions are expanded, and I know with certainty that I will be a mental health advocate for life.

Our challenges and struggles don't define us, our shared humanity does. What we do for others when we lend a hand or a listening ear is the most beautiful part of being human. It's putting the *we* before *me*. This book is intended to connect us, to help make us laugh, and remind us that we are stronger together. So, find a comfy spot to read and let laughter come to the surface this time; I know we all need it!

To Learn More About #SameHereGlobal

www.xfactoredu.org/samehere

Internationally recognized as a digital citizenship expert, Dr. Marialice B.F.X. Curran is an author, consultant, and speaker who is the global connector behind the Digital Citizenship Institute (https://www.digcitinstitute.com). Committed to Human-Centered Design, Dr. Curran leads by hand, heart, and mind as she models how to make a positive impact in local, global, and digital communities. She has served as an associate professor and middle school teacher and principal. As a connected educator and community architect, her work with school communities around the world has created positive and powerful shifts in how we engage and learn online.

#StrongerTogether

YOU'RE MUTED

By Kim Zajac

You're Muted.
Can you please mute yourself?
Umm...*You're NOT muted.*
Your camera is on.

The human condition is centered in reality... just as collaboration and communication are solidly centered through "meetings" on any educator's calendar. We have all been there– and we will continue to go there. Imperfectly perfect in the ways we do.

There are no words that more clearly point these truths out than– "You're Muted."; "Can you please mute yourself?"; "Umm...You're NOT muted."; "Your camera is on."

Who has not had these words directed at them? Who has not offered these words to the others in the room? Who has had to use these words outside of a virtual meeting room (as a gentle nudge) because... the need was there in a real life meeting?

How we work together within these spaces we share- in real life or virtually- relies heavily on our ability to stay grounded in humility-driven human-centeredness as well our skillfulness for pairing the collective passion to do good and make an impact in a way that honors everyone involved.

2

To this end, we must appreciate the following:

"People arrive when and how they can." (Kim Zajac, July, 2023)

I believe this because... I have been in the room where it happens.

The range of unexpected experiences in my years of practice can not be measured. What I can offer is a sampling of the truths that have pushed me to see people for who they are – arriving when and how they can– helping me to grow as a professional and as a human being. I extend deepest gratitude to— all the bumpy entrances I observed where emotions are driving the literal and figurative bus or when fingers are being waved in the air with confused inquiries- "What are YOU doing here?!", all the crying children in the background who in one moment stirred both compassion and distraction, all the parents squeezing in a virtual meeting "on the job" multitasking from start to finish juggling anything from keyboards to paint rollers while jockeying for optimal workplace locations for wifi and privacy.

There will be times we will need to call on our human ability to relate and laugh WITH (not at) the people in the room over any other skill in our professional toolbox. This is how we call people in (the opposite of calling someone out) to do the work and meet the goals we seek to reach– together.

In normalizing the bumpy entrances, joining meetings in costume with accessories because it happens to be a spirit day at school, or embracing any other nuanced or eyebrow-raising delivery, we honor each other as human beings. We see each other as human beings who arrive when and how we can; who have more similarities than differences and who at the core share a capacity to care, empathize, laugh and do hard things better together and for the future.

It's time for me to mute myself. It is my hope that this can sit with you in a way that makes you laugh, cry and experience a "same here" moment.

Kim (@ZajacSLP) is a certified Speech/Language Pathologist and Audiologist in Massachusetts. She is an affiliated virtual practicum instructor at Emerson College in the Speech@Emerson Graduate Program. Kim is a MassCUE board member, Co-leader of the Conference Committee, Co-Leader of the MassCUE Inclusive Learning SIG. Kim is a Co-Founder of @EdCampSoutheasternMA. Kim is a Vital Prize Challenge Educator Mentor and an Adobe Creative Educator Leader. She has presented at SXSWEDU, ISTE, MassCUE, Deeper Learning Conference, NELMS Annual Conference, and NYC

Schools Tech Summit. She has been a guest on MassCUE Get A CUE Podcast, Stronger Together Podcast as well as the Linked up: Breaking Boundaries In Education Podcast. With over 25 years of experience working with individuals across a variety of settings, Kim specializes in creating programs and sharing learning strategies to support students with diverse learning needs. She is passionate about establishing equitable access and inclusion for ALL students.

HERE WE GO

And here we go. What is this? Is this a book? Well, it is printed words on pages. However, when I think about it, it's more like hanging out in a social space, wherever that may be for you, and talking with a collection of educators who have had years in the classroom, creating smiles and sharing knowledge. I think of an educator shaking their head because they can't wait to share a story that they know will make the other person say, "You can't make that up."

Some of these stories may seem unbelievable unless you're in education. And that's not just teachers but anyone who walks through those schoolhouse doors every day in any capacity in a school.

My name is Matt, or if you want to be formal, Dr. Matthew X. Joseph. I am not the author of this book, but I am pulling it all together. Why, you ask? Because we all need to laugh a little bit more. This journey of education, it's not one they teach you in school.

A school year is about 180 days that anything can happen, and most days, "it" does happen, whatever "it" is. That's 180 days of a job that so many of us love and, at the same time, frustrates us more often than we want to admit.

For me, my path into this field has been anything but ordinary. I started as a physical education major at Springfield College. I love my school, and I bleed maroon to this day. I even have a Springfield College tattoo. The heartbeat of SC is the humanities philosophy, a strong spirit, mind, and body.

I quickly realized that being a physical education teacher, even though I loved it and wanted to do it, could be a challenge for a career. On the first day of my Practicum, the principal looked at me when I walked in the door, beaming with pride with my Springfield College shirt and maroon shorts, and he just pointed and said, "The gym is down there, buddy." I knew right then that wouldn't be my profession for the next 40 years. I have the utmost respect for physical education educators; still to this day, two of my best friends are physical education teachers. But I changed my major that day to an elementary school teacher and was an elementary school teacher for the first 15 years of my career. And then, as often happens in this profession, I was promoted to a totally different job.

Education is one of the only professions I know of where doing a job well gets you a new job that has nothing to do with the job you just had. So then, I spent the next ten years as an elementary school principal and the past eight as a district leader. And in true transparency, as this book will be, my journey has not been the smoothest of rides with changing jobs, having multiple jobs cut because of budgets, COVID, bad bosses, and so on. So it's been vital for me to connect with others, laugh, and stay positive during this journey that education is on. I know many of us have faced similar challenges and struggles during our careers, and shared hardships are the foundation of #SameHere, to empower us to share and know we are not alone.

So what is this? Educators from across the globe contributed to a collection of stories because they, like me, believe in this field but also believe we need to laugh more. I started with a podcast named "You Can't Make This Sh*t up" to laugh during COVID and now I'm taking some of those stories and some new ones and creating this book.

Also, in the true spirit of conversational moments, the stories are going to be just straight, raw conversation like it would be in the staff room or at your favorite restaurant or bar. A lot of "so" and "and," and the formatting will be slightly different. OH WELL. Sure, you might see some mistakes. Sure, there will be some things that might sound jumbled. Is this the most professional thing to not make it "look" right? Probably not. But this profession is messy and unpredictable.

I will also be sharing at least one story, if not two, to contribute to the project.

LAUGHING TOGETHER

I hope this book will give individuals a little laughter and smiles. I wanted to share some unbelievable times in this profession and elicit some disbelief and/or laughter. Over my 11 years as a teacher, 10 as a principal, and 8 in the central office, I have worked with thousands of students and hundreds of adults. Individuals have specific needs and often have uncontrollable actions. The goal of sharing stories is not to "make fun" or poke anyone or any issue. The contributors of this book are high-level professional educators who care for kids and love their job.

We share humorous stories that are meant to engage and entertain the reader. Naturally, we want laughter to fill a room, and we share your enjoyment of our words. However, the stories' laughter or "jokes" are never towards specific individuals or disabilities, and are never meant to cause discomfort or hurt feelings.

As an educator, I always strive to foster an inclusive and respectful environment. Laughter is a beautiful tool for building connections and enhancing the learning experience. Still, it is equally essential that it is inclusive and not targeted at anyone negatively. We want all students to feel comfortable, respected, and valued in our classroom community.

As a school/district leader, I share these messages with the school community about having fun but always being mindful of individuals:

Respect and Empathy: We focus on the importance of treating others with respect and empathy. We encourage our community to consider how their words or laughter may affect others and to be mindful of different perspectives and experiences.

Focus on the Content: We understand that laughter should be directed at the humor within the story or situation rather than at individuals or their differences. We encourage our community to appreciate the storyline, wordplay, or comedic elements without excluding or hurting others.

Inclusion and Acceptance: We emphasize the value of embracing diversity and celebrating differences. We encourage our community to appreciate and accept their classmates' unique qualities, abilities, and backgrounds, fostering an environment where everyone feels included and valued.

Open Communication: We communicate openly and respectfully. If anyone in our community witnesses any form of exclusion, teasing, or hurtful behavior in the classroom, they should approach a teacher or a trusted adult to address the issue, ensuring everyone's voices are heard and valued.

I appreciate that educators work together to create a positive and inclusive learning environment in our field. Let us continue to nurture an atmosphere where laughter can flourish, promoting unity, respect, and growth for all students.

IMPORTANCE OF LAUGHTER

Joy and laughter are not mere sources of amusement but essential components of a well-rounded and fulfilling life. They profoundly impact our physical, emotional, and social well-being. By embracing joy and seeking moments of laughter, we can enhance our overall health, strengthen our relationships, and create a more positive and joyful world. Laughter serves several essential functions in human life. Here are some key reasons why we need laughter:

Social Bonding: Laughter helps us connect with others and build social relationships. Shared laughter creates a sense of camaraderie, promotes a positive atmosphere, enhances social bonds, and reduces feelings of loneliness and isolation. It fosters a positive and supportive environment, which is beneficial for mental well-being. It can strengthen friendships, ease tensions, create lasting memories, and foster a sense of belonging and shared joy. Couples who share laughter often report higher relationship satisfaction.

Emotional Well-being: Laughter has a profound impact on our emotional state. It releases endorphins, which are natural feel-good chemicals that promote a sense of happiness and relaxation. Laughing can reduce stress, alleviate anxiety and depression, and improve overall emotional well-being. Laughing also stimulates the production of serotonin, a neurotransmitter associated with feelings of happiness and contentment. It can elevate mood, lift spirits, and provide a natural boost of positivity.

Physical Health Benefits: Laughter has various physical health benefits. It boosts the immune system, increases blood flow, and stimulates the release of beneficial hormones. Regular laughter has been associated with lower blood pressure, reduced pain perception, improved cardiovascular health, and enhanced resilience to illness.

Stress Relief: Laughter is a powerful stress reliever. It helps reduce the levels of stress hormones, such as cortisol, in the body and it promotes relaxation. Laughing can temporarily distract us from stressors, help us gain a new perspective, and provide a mental and emotional release from tension.

Cognitive Function: Laughter can positively affect cognitive functioning and mental agility. It stimulates the brain, improves creativity and problem-solving abilities, and enhances memory and learning. When we laugh, we become more open-minded and receptive to new ideas, leading to increased productivity and improved cognitive performance.

Psychological Resilience: Humor and laughter are crucial in building psychological and emotional resilience. They help us cope with difficult situations, bounce back from setbacks, and maintain a positive outlook on life. Laughing at challenging circumstances can provide a sense of empowerment and help us find meaning and perspective in adversity.

Communication and Humor: Laughter is an important component of human communication. It helps us convey lightheartedness, establish rapport, and engage in playful interactions. Humor and laughter can break down barriers, diffuse conflicts, and promote effective communication and understanding.

Incorporating laughter into daily life and seeking opportunities for humor and joy can contribute to overall mental well-being and relieve life's challenges.
So why are we laughing at education? Well, WHY NOT! The profession of education can be funny for several reasons:

Interaction with Students: Teachers often find humor in the unpredictable and amusing things students say. Children have a unique perspective on the world, and their innocence and curiosity can lead to unexpected and humorous situations in the classroom.

Humor as a Teaching Tool: Incorporating humor into teaching can make learning more engaging and enjoyable for students. Teachers may use jokes, funny anecdotes, or humorous examples to help students understand and remember information. Finding creative and amusing ways to present educational content can add fun to the classroom.

Classroom Dynamics: The dynamics among students and between the teacher and students can create humorous moments. Students may make witty remarks, engage in playful banter, or respond in funny ways during class discussions. Teachers often have stories of amusing interactions and situations that arise during their teaching experiences.

Unexpected Situations: Teaching involves working with diverse groups of students, each with their unique personalities, strengths, and quirks. Teachers may encounter unexpected situations, such as students accidentally saying something funny, spontaneous reactions to activities, or amusing misunderstandings. These moments can bring laughter and fun to the classroom.

Shared Experiences: Teachers often share their funny or relatable experiences with their colleagues, creating a sense of camaraderie and bonding. They can swap stories, exchange humorous anecdotes, and find solace in the fact that they are not alone in encountering funny situations in their profession.

Dealing with Challenges: Humor can also serve as a coping mechanism for teachers when faced with the profession's challenges. Laughing about difficult situations or finding humor amid stressful times can help alleviate tension, reduce stress, and maintain a positive outlook.

It's important to note that while education can be funny, the profession also involves significant responsibilities, hard work, and dedication. Humor is just one aspect of the multifaceted world of education that can bring joy, create connections, and make the learning experience more enjoyable for everyone involved.

If This Chalkboard Could Talk

IF THIS
CHALKBOARD
COULD TALK

STORIES FROM GLOBAL EDUCATORS TO MAKE
YOU LAUGH, CRY, SHAKE YOUR HEAD AND
SAY . . .

YOU CAN'T MAKE THIS UP

A QUICK LAUGH

Good morning Mrs. Bemis, my son only had 2 hours of sleep last night.

Goooood luck.

Christine Bemis
Grade 2 Teacher
@ChristineBemis2

A QUICK LAUGH

Mr. Joseph, I solved the math problem – we should just ask the calculator to do our homework, and we can all take a nap.

Matthew Joseph
Grade 3
Pittsfield, MA

NOT DOTS

By Mary Howard

We've all had that moment in education where we've just finished giving directions to students, and invariably a hand goes up asking, "what are we doing?" This is a story about a time when I had just finished giving specific directions, and things took a wrong turn. You see, I'm a science teacher, and teaching science comes with its own mix of frustration due to the fact that safety and following directions are of particular importance. On this day, we were working with Calcium Chloride to examine its properties. In Western New York, Calcium Chloride is in abundant supply. If you're unfamiliar, Calcium Chloride is used to melt ice, and it looks like small, round, white, pebbles similar to bird seed in size.

Preparing to release the students to work in their groups, I had just finished my safety lecture, letting them know that they needed to wear gloves and goggles to handle the Calcium Chloride and that they needed to be careful not to spill it and, OF COURSE not to eat it. I asked the students if there were any questions. No one had any questions. Students were to be working in small groups; the steps in the process were demonstrated AND printed out at each station. It seemed like everybody understood the directions and expectations, or so I thought. It wasn't even one minute after I'd finished explaining that I heard a student declare, "Oh look at this....it's Dippin' Dots" and she subsequently licked her finger and tried to dip it in the cup to taste the "Dippin' Dots" (Calcium Chloride.) Fortunately, I was able to stop her in time. And no my dear girl, it's NOT dots.

Mary is the author of Artificial Intelligence to Streamline Your Teacher Life: ChatGPT Guide For Educator. She is also a Nationally Board Certified Teacher and teaches 6th grade ELA and Science in Grand Island, New York. She has found success using digital tools that not only make learning fun for her students, but encourage critical thinking, collaboration, and create a life-long passion for learning. Whether the digital experience is related to Science, Technology, Engineering, Mathematics or promotes literacy, Mary believes passionately in the potential that technology has for reaching and engaging ALL learners. In pursuit of this passion.

FORGETFUL STUDENT
By Mike Earnshaw

Being a principal for eight years, an assistant principal for two, and then teaching for nearly 15 years, I mean, there's tons of stories. But there is one that I just don't think I'll ever forget and it actually happened about two years ago.

So this was a time when I was getting out of my office and into classrooms. I had my mobile desk and was out in the halls. I was eating lunch in the cafeteria; I was never in the front office. My focus was always to be around the kids.

There was this one student, and we all have this one student in our lives, who was just full of questions. Every time you see them, they've got a question. And it can go one of two ways: You can be having the kind of day where you're like, *I need to go see so and so, because I just need a good laugh.* Or it's the kind of day where you got too much going on, and you're like, *Oh, no, there they are. I got to go the other way.*

So on this day, I didn't have 30 minutes to talk. I came out of the office and I was going to head to a classroom. I went out the back door and by the back door, there's a set of bathrooms that aren't used very often because there's not many classrooms there.

So I see this student and I'm having a great day. I got some time; I'm just going to hang out in someone's room. The student comes out, and he starts talking to me. I'm asking him how his day's going. He's asking me if I'm going to go to the bathroom. I'm like, "No. If I'm using the bathroom, I use the staff bathroom." I thought it was an odd question for him to ask; thanks for checking on me.

In addition to his questions, this kid also has an obsession with IDs, like staff IDs. Now, at the elementary level, we don't give our students their student IDs. We keep them in the library and the teachers have a set for when students get hot lunch. So every time he would see me, he'd grab my lanyard, and flip through my IDs; for some reason, I keep, like, five years of pictures with me.

He's flipping through, looking, and making comments like, "Oh, you looked younger here. Where's your hair here?" We're talking and it's probably been about 15-20 minutes at this point. Finally, I'm like, "Alright, well, you better get back to class. I'm sure your teacher is wondering where you are."

And he's like, "Okay," and he kind of runs away. I barely make a move and I see him come running back. I'm say to him, "Hey, what are you doing? Did you forget something in there?"

He's says he didn't. Now you see someone running back into the bathroom, right? There's a couple of responses I would expect to hear. I expect, "Oh, I left the bathroom pass in there." Or, "Oh, I left my pen," or "I forgot to wash my hands." But none of those, none of those are his response. As he's running, he doesn't even stop. Instead, he goes, "No, I forgot to wipe my butt!"

I'm thinking, how do you forget to wipe your butt? And then two, he's just been all over my lanyard. He's been touching me.

Before the pandemic, I was all about fist bumps and high fives and giving hugs. I'm thinking, if he forgot to do that, I guarantee his hands weren't washed. Who knows what he's been doing? I'm sitting in the hall, I'm just like, "Hey, make sure you wash your hands when you're done!"

I went back into the office, and disinfected my lanyard, my ID, I washed my hands, and I don't even think I went back to a classroom that day. I was traumatized.

Michael Earnshaw (@MikeREarnshaw) is a father, husband, & the 2023 Illinois South Cook Elementary Principal of the Year! He is the author of The EduCulture Cookbook: Recipes & Dishes to Positively Transform School & Classroom Culture with EduMatch Publishing & co-host of the Punk Rock Classrooms Podcast. Michael strives to empower others to know they can change the world by fostering positive, trusting relationships & modeling risk-taking himself. When he's not helping others & changing lives you can find him skateboarding, running, & creating smiles.

WHAT'S YOUR NAME?

By Aimee Bloom

Young kids say the cutest things, and sometimes the most remarkable moments are when they're misunderstood. I spent about 12-15 years in the classroom. I started my career in art, and then made my way to computer science and digital literacy, where I taught preschool through 8th grade for many years. At the beginning of the year, I always, just like most educators do, find it really valuable to get to know each one of my students.

But my favorite was preschool. So I would sit on the carpet with them, and we would all talk, and I would have them introduce themselves. Four-year-olds are all excited. They go around the room. This one year I'll never forget.

I'm telling them about myself and we're going around, and we get to this one student, and I ask his name.

His reply: Jack Ass.

And I sat there, and I was like, what's your name?

Again he says, Jack Ass.

And I'm like, okay. Now I'm panicking and looking around the room, not knowing there's another Jack because I didn't know this yet. And the preschool teacher is, like, gazing off because she's probably heard everybody's favorite color and their third favorite dinosaur.

But I'm sitting there, and I'm looking at the child, and I'm like, say your name again. And he is, all proud, sits up. Jack Ass.

I cannot do this anymore, and then I looked at the teacher and ask, "What is his name?" She asks, "What did he say it was?"
So I respond with "Jack Ass."

She belly laughs and says his last name, Smith, and I swear to you, I thought the kid was calling himself Jack Ass. But was saying Jack S.

Jack what?

As the Supervisor for Instructional Technology at the Buffalo Public School District, Aimee (@AJBloom2pnto) has over 18 years of experience in education. Her career began as a PreK-8th grade art and computer teacher, where her role quickly expanded into assisting educators with educational technology, Website design, and data management.

BLOOD OR VOMIT

By Carl Hooker

When I first started teaching, I was moved from teaching 5th grade to 1st grade and had one day to learn the difference. Needless to say it was a mess. After a couple of weeks the nurse came to me and said "you've got to quit sending every kid with a stomach ache to the office". I didn't know how 6-year olds operated, so I instituted a rule. I have to see blood or vomit for them to go to the nurse. About a semester in, it all back-fired.

I was doing some small group re-teaching at a table while the other students worked independently. This extremely shy student named Ashley came over and started tugging on the sleeve of my shirt to tell me something. I told her I would get to her in a second but before I could even finish, I felt the warm ooze all down the side of my arm. *I stood up and the class looked at me in shock to which I said ....*

She can go to the nurse!

Carl (@mrhooker) has been an educator for the past 21 years. He has held a variety of positions in multiple districts, from 1st-grade teacher to Virtualization Coordinator.

He speaks on a multitude of topics from thoughtful technology integration with mobile devices to strategies on how to utilize flexible furniture in the classroom. He is the author of Ready. Set, FAIL! And has a 6-part book series titled *Mobile Learning Mindset*. He's also a national advisor for the Future Ready Schools Initiative. He blogs regularly at his blog HookEDonInnovation.com

WARDROBE CHANGE

By Chris Jones

So that story was more like the, *Oh, my God, deflating* story. The next one is the *You can't believe these things actually happen* story. I'm at a different school, and I'm the principal in the main office and girls at the school tend to wear these really short shorts. Honestly, they're more like bikini bottoms than shorts.

A teacher calls down to the office and says, "Look, we can't have this," and blah, blah, blah, "So she's being called down to the office." So, the student is coming down because she has really short shorts on and at the same time, unbeknownst to us, her mother is coming in to drop something off because the daughter called her.

The student's mother comes in to drop this thing off, but she doesn't know what's going on with her daughter's shorts. The main office secretary looks at the mother and goes, "Oh, it's a good thing you stopped by. We have your daughter coming down."

The mother goes, "Yeah, I know. I'm dropping this stuff off."

"No," says the secretary, "She was just sent to the office."

"What are you talking about?" asks the mother. "What for?"

So, in walks the daughter to the main office. She says hi to her mom and then walks by the front desk to go to the main office secretary. As the girl turns the corner and passes her mother, her mother sees what she's wearing on her lower half. Instantly, the mother starts screaming at her. Now we're in the middle of the whole thing, and the mother starts screaming at her about being a slut. She's body shaming her daughter about being too fat to be wearing those shorts. It just turns into a crazy scene. And as if it can't get any worse, the mother goes, "Is that your bathroom?" and points to the bathroom in our main office.

We say, "Yeah."

So she takes her daughter into the bathroom. The door shuts, and the whole time, outside, you can hear swearing and F bombs across the whole front office into the main hallway. The mother is yelling at her about these shorts and everything.

So a minute, maybe two, passes; it felt more like 20. And the daughter comes walking out, and is now wearing the mom's pants. No word of a lie. The daughter's wearing the mom's pants.

The mom comes out of the bathroom, can't get the shorts on that the daughter was wearing, so she's got the daughter's shorts in one hand, and some shirt or something that she had, like a sweatshirt, half wrapped around her lower half.

She's literally in her underwear and she's swearing at her daughter about how now she's late for work because she was dressed for work and now she's not. And how she can't believe she has to deal with this. The mother is just swearing the whole time. Walking out, the mother is like, "How do you like it now?! Your mom's walking around with her butt hanging out!"

I'm like, *Really?* There's people in the main office watching all this happen. We're at a point where we're sitting with our mouths open. *Is this really happening?*

And now all we can do is get the mother out as soon as possible because the only thing that would be worse is if the bell rings and she's walking out during passing time.

Dr. Chris Jones (@DrCSJones) has been an educator in Massachusetts for 22 years. He has just finished his 14th year as a building administrator. Chris is currently the President-Elect of the Massachusetts State Administrators Association (MSAA) and Principal of Whitman-Hanson Regional High School in Massachusetts. He is the author of SEEingtoLead, a book that provides strategies for how modern leaders can and must support, engage, and empower their teachers to elevate student success. He also hosts a podcast of the same name to amplify teachers' voices in an effort to improve education as a whole.

Chris is passionate about continuous improvement and the idea that success is not a destination, but a process. This can be seen in the presentations and workshops he has given for the Massachusetts School Administrators Association (MSAA), Massachusetts Computer Using Educators (MassCUE), Massachusetts Association of Supervision and Curriculum Development (MASCD), the Association of Supervision and Curriculum Development (ASCD), and the National Association of Secondary School Principals (NASSP).

Most recently, Chris was a finalist for the Massachusetts School Administrators Association's Principal of the Year award and named the 2022 Massachusetts School Counselors Associaltion's (MASCA) Administrator of the Year. Chris' education includes a BA from Bridgewater State University, an MA from Salem State University, and a Doctorate from Northeastern University. He currently resides in Southeastern Massachusetts with his wife, Mary (Bella) and two boys, Tommy and Scotty.

LOCK'EM UP

Ever had a 3rd grader plan a field trip for you? Well I did and one with the honorable Judge Lindsay who found one of my students guilty in a mock trial and put him in a holding cell (Glad his mother was a

Dr. Rayna Freedman (@rlfreedm) is a 5th grade teacher at the Jordan/Jackson Elementary School in Mansfield, MA. She has taught grades 3-5. Rayna is the Past President of MassCUE. Rayna has presented at various conferences worldwide. She believes in student agency and the power of building relationships and community.

FLUFFY

By Christine Ravesi-Weinstein

As anyone who's been an administrator in a school knows, you're like a Swiss Army knife. Stuff happens, and you've just got to go with it, like the day I met Fluffy.

A staff member came down to my office and said, "I really need someone to help. The math teacher down the hall is freaking out. There's a lizard in her room."

I was stunned, "There's there's what? There's a student with a lizard?"

"Yes!" The teacher was very stressed out.

It was one of those things where you contemplate how your life ended up here. You start to question all those little decisions you made. If I had done this or that, would I currently be sitting in this office figuring out what to do with a lizard?

According to the messenger, the teacher was freaking out. She doesn't like lizards. And in my head, I'm thinking, *Some people do?* I have so many questions: Is it running around the room? Is it hanging out on the desk? Is it like a gecko? What kind of a lizard is this?

So I do what everyone who's been trained to be an administrator does. I text the rest of the admin team, saying, "Ms. So and so has a live lizard in class, what do we do? Lizard emergencies were not part of my principal preparation class."

And so my principal replied, "Of course she does. Get the student and the lizard and have the kid call a parent to come pick up the lizard. And take a picture of the kid with the lizard and send it to us."

I'm like, "Okay."

I walk down to the room, and the teacher is in the hall, shaking and crying, saying, "I can't be in the room." I ask, "What's going on?" She responds, "That student in the second row, third seat back, has a lizard."

I peek my head into the room. I don't see a lizard. I'm expecting to see it on the desk. "Where is it?" I ask.
She says, "It's down her shirt!"

I was like, "Excuse me. It's, like, down her hoodie? How do you know the lizard's there?"
She responded, "It's poking out of the hoodie on her neck."

I can't do this. I didn't sign up for this. But I can't leave this teacher hanging. So I walk into the room, walk up to the student, and say, "Do you have a lizard?" She's like, "Yeah." I reply, "Can you grab your stuff and come with me? You can't have a lizard."

Of course, the lizard had a name, and it wasn't like what you'd think. Not, Scaly, or Oscar. It was like Fluffy or something. She is telling me she always has Fluffy with her.

Now I'm like, "Okay, whatever."

She comes out of the room, and I tell her she needs to go to my office. I walk with the student and Fluffy to my office and text the admin team, "Fluffy's with me. It's legit a lizard. It's approximately two and a half feet long."

It's a bearded dragon, but because I don't do reptiles, it's like a Komodo dragon to me. Now the girl starts stroking it and petting it.

The rest of the admin team comes down, and they're all marveling at Fluffy, too. They were saying things like, "You're not kidding. It's a legit lizard."

We start asking the students questions.
"Does Fluffy come to school often?" She replies, "Usually once a week."

"How has no one ever seen Fluffy before?" She replies, "Because I carry him around in my hoodie like this."
"Do students know Fluffy's in school?" She replies, "Yeah."

At this point, I say, "You know Fluffy can't be here, right? Like, Fluffy needs to go home, so can we call Mom to pick up Fluffy?"

I took a picture of Fluffy because I was told to do that. And then called mom. The student went outside and met Mom. Mom took the bearded lizard home.

I told the student, "Unless it's, like, a certified therapy lizard with a vest, it can't be here in school."

So I guess I learned that day we need official lizard protocol.

Christine Ravesi-Weinstein currently serves as a high school Assistant Principal in Massachusetts, USA and previously worked as a high school science department chair for four years and classroom teacher for 15. Diagnosed with anxiety and depression at 23, Christine began her journey toward mental wellness. She began a non-profit organization in June of 2017 aimed at removing the stigma of mental illness and promoting physical activity as a means to cope with anxiety.

As an avid writer and educator, Christine became passionate about bridging the two with her advocacy for mental health.Christine has presented at numerous national conferences and has provided professional development for educators in various districts. Follow her work on Twitter @RavesiWeinstein and on YouTube at http://bit.ly/TheRunnersHigh. For more information about Christine, please visit her website at www.ravesiweinstein.com

MAX'S GAS

By Mrs. Jen Jenkins

There was a mischievous fifth-grader named Max. Max was known for his love of pranks and unstoppable humor. He could turn even the most mundane situations into laughter-filled adventures. One day, Max found himself in a situation that would leave his classmates roaring with laughter.

It was a warm Monday morning when Max's class gathered for their daily lessons. Mrs. Jenkins, their teacher, was explaining the intricacies of math, her voice as soothing as a lullaby. As the minutes ticked by, the room became quieter and quieter, and Max's temptation for mischief grew stronger.

Suddenly, Max felt an unexpected rumble deep within his stomach. He knew the signs all too well – it was the dreaded gas monster that had been dwelling inside him since breakfast. Max saw an opportunity for unforgettable hilarity as his classmates focused on their math problems.

Suppressing a mischievous grin, Max concocted a brilliant plan in his mind. He leaned to one side, pretending to tie his shoelaces, and just as Mrs. Jenkins was explaining a complex equation, he released the pent-up gas with the force of a rocket launch.
The classroom fell silent for a split second, the momentary pause pregnant with anticipation. Then, an unmistakable sound erupted—a loud, trumpet-like toot echoed throughout the room. The class froze in disbelief, their eyes darting from Max to Mrs. Jenkins, who was momentarily stunned into silence.

Max, however, was a master of improvisation. He transformed his gas-induced predicament into a symphony of comedy in one swift motion. He raised his hand dramatically and exclaimed, "Mrs. Jenkins, it wasn't me! My shoe just made a musical statement about the importance of math in our lives! It's a spontaneous math-ic! See, even my shoes can't resist the magic of numbers!"

The class erupted into laughter, their initial shock replaced with uproarious amusement. Mrs. Jenkins, unable to keep a straight face, joined in the laughter, her eyes twinkling with amusement.

From that day forward, Max became a legend in his class. The tale of the "math-ic" incident spread like wildfire, turning a potentially embarrassing moment into a legendary act of comedy. Max's classmates never forgot the day their friend brought a symphony of laughter to their otherwise ordinary math lesson.

And so, the legend of Max, the fifth-grader who turned a simple toot into a comedic masterpiece, was passed down from one class to another, ensuring that his mischievous spirit and unyielding sense of humor would be remembered for years to come.

A QUICK LAUGH

In the middle of class, one kid yelled out.......

Who let the dogs out, Whoot Whoot Whoot Whoot

He then looked around the classroom and very genuinely apologized and said, **"*just needed to get it out. It was doing no good inside.*"**

Grade 5 Teacher
Nashville, TN

IT'S ABOUT TO GO DOWN

By Matthew X. Joseph

I was about twenty-four years old, it was my first year in public school. I taught in a private school for two years right out of college, but I was still a fetus as far as teaching goes.

It was my first parent/teacher conference. I did student teaching and practiced these parent conferences; my mentor also got me ready. I looked at the list of parents participating, and I noticed the first one was people I knew from high school. *Okay, this is going to be smooth.*

The couple were high school sweethearts, and I know them, so to get off the ground, this is going to be an easy one, right? Well, let me tell you.

So the father comes walking in, let's call him Brian. And I was like, "Hey, Brian, what's up, man? I can't wait to talk about your son."

Brian greets me and says, "I gotta warn you, my wife's bringing a friend."

"Okay, that's cool." So I'm sitting there, and his wife comes walking in, and she's pregnant.

So I turned to Brian and said, "Hey, congratulations. Didn't know that you were having a baby." The problem was, I didn't see the wife's friend behind her, and he said, "That's my baby."

Brian immediately stands up and says, "We don't know that yet." So this isn't the wife's friend, it's the wife's boyfriend. So I tried to change the subject and said, "Hi, everybody, can we just sit down? Let's talk about the student. I have all this data here..." and Brian and the boyfriend were still staring each other down like they're in a WWE ring. So I turn my attention to the wife, Sue.

"Hey, Matt, nice to see you," she's being sweet as if nothing's happening around us. There's her, and two men, one her husband, and she's still wearing her wedding ring, and then the boyfriend.

So now I'm like, there's only two chairs. Not that we couldn't find another chair, but it was just a little awkward. So the boyfriend grabs a chair, sits down, and I'm still stunned.

I tried to restart the meeting a second time, "Let's talk about Brian Jr.."

The dad tells Sue, "I don't feel comfortable with your boyfriend here."

And Sue says, "Just because you're my husband doesn't mean I can't have a boyfriend."

Now I'm stuck in my tracks; is this happening? I'm sitting here with a dad, his wife, and his wife's boyfriend, and she's pregnant with one of their baby.

I started going through the paperwork and going through the information, and as I got close to the end, I said, "Okay, would you like me to send home two reports?" Everybody looks confused. Are you ready for this? They all lived in the same house. Now I am just dumbfounded.

"Hold on a second," I said. I couldn't help myself. "Brian, you and your wife live together." And they said, "No, all three of us live together."

This was in 1997. and I think *this was not in the student handbook. This was not part of my task to get my certification. This was not how the first conference was supposed to go.*

As we went to wrap it up, I said, "Any questions?" And I looked right at Brian. But the boyfriend says, "I have a question."

I look over like. "Why is he here?" And he pointed at Brian.

"I don't know. He's the dad. I think it's appropriate that he's here."

And Brian said, "Why are you here?" pointing at the boyfriend.

"Okay, our ten minutes are up. We're going to wrap this up," I said. But they wouldn't leave because then it got into a contest of who would leave first: Brian or the boyfriend?

As for me? I just walked out. I didn't know what to do.

Dr. Matthew X. Joseph
CEO of X-Factor
@MatthewXJoseph

ADULT FLAVORS

By Stephanie Howell

This story takes place close to the end of the school year. This past year I was coaching a teacher.

We had weekly meetings in the calendar where we just met and talked about instructional strategies to improve her teaching. On this day, we were meeting, g, and then we would co-teach later in the day. But between the first and second meetings, I had to run to another building because I was assigned to five different buildings in our district. I had to go to another building quickly, and then I would come back and co-teach with this teacher.

So I went to the other building, met with another teacher, and then I got a text from her, what kind of Kona Ice do you want? I texted back that I wanted strawberry. I was excited because that sounded great. The PTO bought this ice machine, and the principal was doing great things to reward students at the end of the year. Everybody was celebrating and using the Kona Ice maker.

After she read my text that I said I wanted strawberry. I get a call from the teacher, and she says, to my surprise, "But we have adult flavors." I looked at my watch, and it was only eleven. Not that the time mattered, we were at work.

I was stunned and said, "I just want strawberry." Because she was in the class and needed a quick answer, I quickly answered with the flavor I wanted. But I did ask, "What do you mean adult flavors?" and she wouldn't really give me a clear answer. She just said kids cant have this type.

So I said again, "I just want strawberry." And we hung up. I did not want to press the issue over the phone since she had students in the classroom.

Now I Am driving back to the school, just wanting a strawberry Kona Ice but thinking, "What is the procedure for this? Like, oh my gosh, this teacher is having adult-flavor beverages at school with kids." I am thinking of alcoholic beverages, and I asked myself, "Who at the district office do I need to contact? Who do I need to talk to about this? What is going on? Why did this principal allow this?"

Now I know the principal is a rule follower, so I am still thinking, "What is going on at this school?" I only had two minutes before I got to the school, and it's good that I only had two minutes because I didn't call anyone. When I got to the school, she again asked why I didn't want adult flavors.

I didn't know how to answer and said, "Because we are with kids."
Now her face was confused, and she said, "What are you talking about?
I felt pressured and blurted out, "Like adult flavors. Alcohol added into our Kona Ice."
Let me tell you, she was dying laughing. She said, "No, Steph, that's not what that means."

I then ask, "What do you think adult flavors mean?" And of course, the principal was there and said, "Oh, my gosh. I can't believe that."

It became really funny, kind of at my expense. As it turns out, the kids just had "typical flavors" where the teachers could get premium.

Then I had to joke back in my best teacher voice and said, "Vocabulary is essential to use in this situation when you're able to say there are premium flavors instead of adult flavors."

Now we are eating our Kona Ice, and so we talked about those misconceptions, which can happen a lot in schools. It can happen a lot with our students, these different misconceptions, terms, or vocabulary that we might use.

When I got to the building to see what was happening, they were not serving adult flavors. And again, it was a funny moment. But I think it's essential always to assume the best and don't react without knowing the entire story. Listening to people and then asking additional questions and digging into things allows time and context to areas where we need to understand people better, and it can cause less conflict.

Stephanie (@mrshowell24) is the CEO of Gold EDU, Control the Chaos EDU, and is also the EdTech Lead for the Pickerington Local Schools District. Stephanie has spoken at conferences around the world. Some of her

achievements are being a part of the team named ISTE's Distinguished District, ISTE Top 20 to Watch in 2023, WOSU Leadership Award, a Google Innovator, and PLSD's Innovative Leader award. Stephanie is one of the founding members of Global GEG and Gold EDU. Stephanie has a master's in Curriculum and Instruction and Educational Leadership. Stephanie is a co-host on two podcasts, Get Inspired and Innovative and Control the Chaos EDU. In addition to her roles in the public school system, she is also an adjunct Professor for Ashland University and Best Selling Co-Author of Control the Chaos: Creating Order in the Classroom and Teaching Executive Functioning Skills.

DOUBLE DIPPER

By Deann Poleon

A while back, I taught 10th grade at ELA. Unfortunately, 10th grade was not my favorite class. I loved 9th grade, which makes me just super weird. This particular year, I had a very interesting mixture of students in my room. The crowd was a tough one.

We were reading Midsummer Night's Dream. For this lesson, we were sitting in a circle. I assigned roles, and the circle lets us see everybody's "name". In this class, I had two really tough kids in my room. Like, really tough kids. One was sitting next to me in the circle (TK#1), and one was sitting across from me(TK#2). They're not even friends with each other, just challenging students. And then I have everyone else.

So I'm sitting there, and then suddenly, TK#1 beside me is elbowing me. And says, "I think I'm going to throw up." He says, "Look across from you." I look up. There's a student, not TK#2, but another student across from me who has two fingers digging for gold. Both fingers at the same time, "double dipping."

And here I am, dry heaving because that stuff makes me gag too. So TK#2, sitting across from us realizes something's going on because we are laughing, dry heaving, and gagging.

And TK#1 next to me nods in the direction of the kid picking his nose. So TK#2 looks, and he sees the "double dipping" in progress and immediately looks like he is going to throw up for real.

So, TK#2, who I never would picture him bothered, had to run out of my room because he was gagging. And now TK#1 and I are laughing because we are dying at the reaction and the boogers that are still being picked.

Who does this happen to? Right? It happens to me.

We went out of the room to check on the student and to get our own selves together. The three of us can't walk back into the room because we have now drawn the whole classroom's attention. And we're dying. We're dying. We're dry heaving, laughing, thinking, "Is this really happening to us?"

We finally gathered ourselves and went back into the room. The whole class is like, "What just happened?" I say, "Yeah, I just had a stomach problem. I had to leave the room for a minute, and these boys were just nice enough to ensure I was okay." And the kids know I was lying but I didn't want to call anyone out (aka the "double dipper"). However, this bonded me with TK#1 and TK#2 for the rest of the school year.

Deann Poleon, a visionary technology integrator in the K-12 education sector, began her professional journey as a high school English teacher before transitioning into the field of technology integration. With a deep passion for education and a strong belief in the power of technology to enhance learning experiences, Deann has made significant contributions to the educational landscape for her district.

SOMETHING IN THE WATER

By Laurie Guyon

Our 6th-grade team would take our students into the Adirondacks for outdoor education. We would sleep in basic cabins, eat in a dining hall and explore the great outdoors for three days.

One of the highlights of our trip every year was to hike up a mountain. It was about a 5-mile hike that is considered moderately challenging. Usually, it took our students about 3 hours to complete. The view at the top made the difficulty worth the time it took to hike. For one student, though, it took much longer because of something out of his control. That year there was something in the water. Several of us were not feeling that well when we started the hike. But, since this is a once-in-a-lifetime opportunity, we all wanted to stay. About an hour into the hike, though, one boy, in particular, was struggling. He was pasty white and a bit clammy. He asked where the bathroom was. Um, the bathroom? We pointed him to go behind a tree and handed him a few tissues. He did what he could and then came back onto the trail. From that point on, up and down the mountain, every 10 minutes, he had to skulk off into the woods to relieve himself. The poor boy had the worst case of diarrhea one could have. Everyone kept telling him it would be ok and sharing their bathroom stories to try and help him not be embarrassed. There was a lot of laughter and sympathy to go around!

Laurie Guyon (@SMILELearning) is the Lead Coordinator for Instructional Technology Programs at WSWHE BOCES in Saratoga Springs, New York. She is the Capital Region Director and a trainer for The New York State Association for Computers and Technologies in Education (NYSCATE). Laurie is also an adjunct professor for SUNY Plattsburgh, where she teaches Digital Age Learning in the CAS SBL program. She is the author of *SMILE Learning: Leveraging the Power of Educational Technology.*

AN UNEXPECTED CLASS VISITOR
By Kevin Leichtman

So as a teacher, I was really closed in. I stayed in my room, I stayed in my space. I did many crazy things, but I never really went around the campus. I didn't know what was happening in the school, on the campus as a whole.

I had a group of sophomores, and I was pushing them. They were doing some difficult, difficult literature. I pulled in some African literature. They had never seen that style of storytelling before. And they're telling me, "This is really cool, but it's difficult and it's heavy. Can we do something to make this fun?"

"Sure. Let's brainstorm. Give me some ideas. What do you want to do?"

"We're in Florida. Can we go outside and do this, maybe?"

I'm thinking to myself, *I've never taken a class outside. Yeah, why not?* "Let me run it by my principal. I'll schedule it out." This was the first and would be the last time I ever took a class of students outside.

So we get there, and I've got this stellar lesson plan. We had a picnic area at the school. I'm like, we can lounge while we do this. It's going to be a beautiful day.

I get there in the morning. It's the first period; we go outside. It's a little cold. People are kind of shivering a little bit, but it's going smoothly enough.

That period ends, and I'm reflecting. If it was a little warmer, it would have been perfect. The second period starts, and we go outside again. The sun is shining. This had to be the best lesson I ever taught. Everybody was happy. We're laughing. We're engaged the whole time. My administrators walk by, and they're like, wow, that's a really good teacher. This is the day, but you know what they say when you're riding that wave, you're crashing down.

So I drop off my second period and grabbed my third-period class. I'm getting a little too cocky. I'm just too into it. Everything seemed to be going right. We get outside. They've got their packets, we're reading the story, we're chatting, we're talking about these things. And as I'm in the middle of reading a passage, I hear a scream. I look up, and one of my students is just in a full-out sprint. I'm like, *what just happened? What's going on?* I thought things were going well. And she's yelling, "B!"

And I'm like, *B what?*

Okay, so I should tell you I'm terrified of bees, okay? Terrified, and I'm not even allergic to them. Once I realize there's an actual bee, I'm trying to keep my cool, but I'm not on the inside. I'm panicking and screaming, too, but I'm telling them, "It's just a bee. It's okay. Let's just shift over this way a little bit."

So we calm back down, the girl sits back down, and we're all good, or so I think. All of a sudden, another scream, another all-out sprint. And I'm like, *are you kidding me? Is it the same bee?* But now the whole class is yelling, "Bees!"

Everybody's up looking around. I look up from these papers, and there's, like, 50 bees heading our way. And they're just terrorizing the area. I'm saying, "Walk, don't run. Everybody stay calm. We're going back to the classroom now."

I got maybe two steps and was like, forget this, let's run! I'm running and screaming. The kids are running and screaming. Of course, an administrator is still out there. There are teachers walking by on their planning period, looking at us like, *what the heck is going on out there?*

I am running for dear life, pushing kids out of the way. I gotta get out of there.

We get back to the classroom. Thankfully, everyone's safe, accounted for, no bee stings. Okay, the lesson is over. We're done; we're not doing anything else for the rest of the day.I am not going outside; I'm shaking.

I got to my lunch break and told some teachers about what happened. They're like, "You didn't know about that?"

"Know about what? Giant bees attacking us in the middle of the day."

They start explaining, "There's a farm right next to this school. They use these bees to pollinate whatever they're doing at that farm. They don't sting. They're totally friendly. They don't bother you at all. There's nothing they can actually do to you."

"I don't care what you say. I'm never going outside again."

I don't know how the students didn't know about the bees, either. Every teacher at the school knew except for me, and every time I told that story, they were like, "Duh. That's when they come out." How was this normal to them? Just killer bees, totally fine.

That was the last time I went outside for the rest of my teaching career at that school. If it was lunchtime, I was in the building. I wasn't going anywhere.

Kevin Leichtman (@KevinLeichtman) received his Ph.D. in Curriculum & Instruction from Florida Atlantic University, where he also completed a Master's degree in Curriculum & Instruction.

Kevin has taught for over 10 years, reaching every grade level from 7-12 and college undergraduates. He has created curriculum, professional development, and presented on the topics of mindset, burnout, and equity to teachers and school leaders at local, national, and international stages.

SLAPPING THE MEAT

By Heather Brantley

As a middle school teacher, you are always working to keep your game face on and laughing only after the discipline has happened and everyone has cleared the room. However, on this day, I lost it in front of the kids as I was trying to make a life lesson out of the situation.

Between class periods, I monitored the halls outside my classroom. Unfortunately, I am across the hallway from the middle school boys' bathroom. I was accustomed to horseplay and rowdy bathroom behavior. I was not prepared for this: Andrew came out of the boy's bathroom and said, "Mrs. Brantley, They are slapping the meat in the bathroom." I made eye contact with the other teacher in the hall and asked him to repeat what he just said to ensure I understood him correctly. He repeated the same statement, leading me to go to the bathroom door and ask everyone to exit. As they were coming out, I heard the story of how they were in the bathroom when Brandon tried to give a hoagie to Charles.

During lunch, Charles had said he wanted a hoagie to eat in my classroom so apparently, Brandon obtained the sandwich and decided to make the transaction in the bathroom before going to class, at which time Charles decided he no longer wanted the hoagie. At this point, they took the hoagie apart and started slapping each other with the meat. While sharing the story of how the hoagie came to be in the bathroom, David walked out of the bathroom, and I asked him to stop and wait so that I could determine his involvement in the story. When he stopped and turned toward me, a piece of lunch meat fell from the back of his shirt and hit the hall floor with a loud splat. Trying not to laugh, I explained how the bathroom is not a place for food exchange, and it was not ok to bring food out from the cafeteria. I also said it was never ok to slap your meat in or out of the bathroom. At this point, I was grinning so big that the other teacher had to thank the kids for being honest about what was happening in the bathroom and that it was not the place to play. All the while, Andrew (the reporting student) is standing in the background with a huge smile on his face knowing the initial statement he gave me definitely could have meant something entirely different.   I am thankful that slapping the meat was a hoagie story, and I was not faced with any other situation. This was definitely not bologna - all turkey!

Another day in the life of a Middle School Teacher.

Heather Brantley (@HeatherTechEdu) is an experienced educator and founder of HeatherTechEdu. With a background in instructional design and technology integration, Heather is passionate about helping teachers and students leverage the power of technology to enhance teaching and learning. Through HeatherTechEdu, she provides presentations on AI/AR/VR in the classroom, instructional design services, and educational technology consulting to schools and districts around the country. Heather is currently teaching CTE technology and CEER at Pine Tree ISD.

A QUICK LAUGH

I remember one time when I worked lunch duty, one of my favorite little first grade girls was getting ready to run out to recess. I stopped her and said, "Beth, maybe wash your face before you go out, You have Ketchup on your cheeks."

She took off anyway screaming,

IT'S MY WAR PAINT!

Grade 1 Teacher
New Jersey

A QUICK LAUGH

As a Physical Education teacher we do a lot of activities that are not just games like skills challenges and fitness tests. One year, I had a student who was very bright and was one of my favorite 6th graders ever. We were having our annual mile run test.

So this student sighs and looks at me and says....

So my parents pay taxes, to pay you, and you make me run?

Grade 6 PE Teacher

Rhode Island

THE BEAR NECESSITIES

By Laura Williams

I write this from a place of knowing better. It was my first year in a middle school classroom. And it was the first class of the day, 2nd-period 7th grade Science. This was my whole house class with a handful of students who needed extra support. Because it was my first year, I had a co-teacher, and because it was a full-house class with many needs, I also had a paraeducator. I hope you are imagining a loud and full classroom with lots of wild personalities with three adults to help wrangle the chaos.

Now I loved a challenge, and this was one of my favorite classes. I wanted to reach students that others thought could not be reached. If I could not reach them through engaging Science experiences, then I would use my dazzling wit and personality. I would use my youth for the "cool" advantage.

So I was in it. The train was moving. They say you never get to a smooth operation until at least three years in. Well, this is so true. The whirlwind of that first year left room for mistakes. This was mine that I now laugh about, but at the time was MORTIFIED.

It was the beginning of class, and I forgot to tee-up an engagement video to get us going for the day while I took attendance. I quickly scoured youtube and found what looked to be a cute cartoon that would contribute to our learning in the life sciences. It was about asexual and sexual reproduction and how that contributes to genetic traits passed down to offspring. Dear reader, you know where this is going.

The video started excellently. Science was on point through the lens of cute, furry bears. It was light-hearted and simplified for students. But then it happened. In showcasing the sexual reproduction and recombination to create diversity in phenotypes (i.e., dark brown fur, light brown fur, etc.), the bears engaged in the act of sexual reproduction. What made it worse, surprisingly, was that there was a giant black sensor over the bears, so you couldn't see anything but the sound effect was squeaking, as if you heard a mattress. I never ran faster to the computer to shut it down.

Some students didn't even notice like it was normal, or perhaps their minds were somewhere else. Some looked up at me in concern. Others, particularly the rambunctious boys, lost it. They yelled Oh My god! As they uncontrollably laughed.

I turned it off, and I said sternly (which is surprising to the students to see me stern at this stage of the game), "Well if you can't properly handle this, we aren't going to watch it!". The whole class went silent. The class went on with our planned activities. And that was that... or so I thought.

The second the bell rang, my co-teaching colleague and the paraeducator burst into laughter. I would not hear the end of the bears in science class. You would be surprised how many connections to bears you can find if you are looking for it! I may have had a few ridiculous emails in my inbox about bears periodically from my colleagues and friends throughout the year. Who knew bears would help establish friendships in a new building?

I am very lucky it wasn't worse, and no parents called. You better believe, though, that every movie, video, article, etc. would be closely vetted before distribution from that day forward.

Laura Williams (@mrswilliams21) (MAT, M.ED ELPS) is your resident authentic learning expert, co-facilitates the Iowa Authentic Learning Network for the Iowa AEAs, and is the founder of the Authentic Learning Alliance. She also is a Project Manager on a statewide project board for PK-12 students across Iowa. Over the past 10 years, she's dedicated herself to transforming education through incorporating authentic learning experiences with area partnerships into PK-12 classrooms as an educator, consultant, and 21st Century Learning Specialist. She believes that education can be "the great equalizer" if we can leverage our student's interests and passions.

A QUICK LAUGH

One of my 3rd graders was late and I asked "is everything Ok Randy, why so late?" He looked me straight in the face and said

My mom is a drama queen and had to do her make up three times to "get it right."

Grade 3 teacher
Portland, ME

A QUICK LAUGH

I was teaching about habitats and how animals survive predators. I started talking about cheetahs and one student asked if I could beat a cheetah in a race. I said with a smile, "I never raced one, but maaaaybe."

The class predictably laughs but one student then yells out.....

Ya right, maybe a a fat injured cheetah.

Grade 4 teacher
Austin, TX

WHEN THE WIND BLOWS

By Frank Rudnesky

So in my classroom, I had a file cabinet that I used to put my books on. This was a high school, so the kids were teenagers; 15, 16, and 17? The fire alarm rang, and we went outside to our usual location.

It was a really windy fall day, and you gotta understand I am a mover and a shaker. The bell rings, and it's time to come inside. I put my stuff on the file cabinet and started to teach. The class looks at me, and the first row starts laughing. So there are always moments as a teacher when kids are going to have these inside jokes, and you're going to start thinking, *What the heck are they laughing at?* I don't know. So I go back behind the cabinet, get my stuff, and come out again. Another kid laughs. I'm like, *Man, what's going on?*

Finally, some kid approaches me and says, "Hey, you have a leaf on your pants." So when the wind blew, a left must have blown up and stuck to the front of my pants. You guessed it, right in my front pants zipper. I looked like Adam from Adam and Eve. At that point, I had to make a decision to either be the brunt of the joke and be embarrassed or embrace it and laugh back at myself.

So at that moment, I made a conscious decision that I would be able to laugh at myself as an educator. If not, I would never have a long career as an educator. I went back behind the cabinet, took the leaf off, and boom, ready to teach leafless.

In addition to teaching at the high school and university levels, Dr. Frank Rudnesky (@DrFrankRud) was the principal of Belhaven Middle School in Linwood, New Jersey for a span of two decades. During that time, the school was recognized with numerous local, state, and national awards for leadership, technology influence, excellence in performance, and a positive culture. The school was often used as a visitation site for other educators from as far away as Japan.

WHO'S YOUR MOMMY

By Rob Elia

There was a meeting I wasn't actually part of this meeting, but a coworker was. He was the lacrosse coach, a really loud guy. He's the type of guy you don't see him; you hear him.

He had a student; we'll call her Ashley. Real tough situation. Ashley was not in a good place. She was acting out, cutting, talking back, shouting back, all that kind of stuff. So they call a meeting with Ashley's mom, the counselors, and the administration.

They met in a big conference room, and the lacrosse coach got called in. Everyone is sitting there. He arrives and sits down, and they say, "We've got Ashley's mom here. We're here to talk about Ashley." And he starts going off the rails, right?

So he's looking across the desk, across this big conference desk, and he just starts going off: "Your daughter is the worst kid. I've taught for 20 years, and she is by far the worst, most tough kid ever. She curses at me. I can't take it anymore." As he's going off, administrations' faces are just lighting up.

Like, literally, his finger is up screaming at this lady across the desk. And the best, well worst, part is, he was yelling at the Guidance Counselor. He didn't know who his coworker was. He thought the Guidance Counselor was the mom.

Follow Rob at: @CoachRobEDU

Digital Learning Enthusiast, Star-Ledger Coach of the Year; Former School Dept. Chairperson; Anti-Bullying Specialist, Safety Team Director.

PLAY OF THE GAME

By Lori

My classroom was in an old two-story building when I was teaching preschool special education. A young student in my class was there specifically for speech delays. He grew up on a farm in another community and was four years old.

So one day, we were going out for recess, and I was a little ways behind him. By the time I caught up to him, he was standing on the top step, whipping down his pants and peeing all over the place. The pee was trickling down the steps. He pulled up his pants, and I started talking to him, "Okay, I understand you had to go, but this isn't appropriate because we're in public."

The best part was that the other kids were coming outside for recess, and one of our teachers saw the puddle on the steps trickling down. So we watched her, and she looked up at the building to see where it was coming from. She's looking around and just standing there, convinced there must be a leak in the roof. She eventually went in and told the principal. The look on her face was priceless. To this day, I never did tell her it was my student's pee all over the steps.

And, of course, the student just ran off and started playing; he was the cutest little thing and just so innocent. The other teacher was an older woman getting close to retiring, and she was just mystified. We all just stood there, my associates and I, and finally, we just had to walk away. And the principal, when he came outside, he was kind of baffled by it too. I'm still in touch with him, and I never told him what it was.

Even yesterday, we were doing *Marty's* soccer. My kids designed a soccer field, and then we had our *Marty*'s on the playing field. It was quite difficult for the kids to get *Marty* to where they wanted him to be. They were learning *Marty* could sidestep to kick the ball. He could walk backward, kick it backward, kick it forward.

So it got to a point where four *Marty*'s all just conjoined in the middle, and one of the kids in my group yelled,

Girl POG!

(Play of the game)

So even the little things, the little laughs, we need those. Once the class is over, I feel the pressure of getting paperwork done and all those things, and it weighs on me. But in the classroom, it is just laughing and joking, having fun, coming back together, and learning. We have to make this fun because there are enough other things in the world that aren't so fun.

TESSELLATIONS

By Jaime Donally

I once taught a third-grade math class at a private school where we worked on tessellations. Many third-grade students struggled because they wanted explicit directions on drawing and coloring their tessellation pages to create patterns.

They had difficulty being creative and demonstrating their understanding of the concept. One student asked me why he was having a hard time, and to my surprise, he asked me ....

Can you define testicles?

The class erupted in laughter, and I explained that I couldn't answer that question and that he should speak to his parents about it. It was a funny moment in the class when the topic of tessellations took a completely different turn.

Jaime (@JaimeDonally) is a passionate technology enthusiast. She began her career as a math teacher and later moved into Instructional Technology. Her desire to build relationships has brought about opportunities to collaborate with students and educators worldwide. She provides staff development and training on immersive technology as an edtech consultant.

Her latest adventures include the launch of Global Maker Day and the #ARVRinEDU community, events, and presentations. She works as an author and speaker to provide practical use of augmented and virtual reality in the classroom.

MEET VIRGINIA

By Bryan Zevotek

How could this chaotic activity be in the plans for a first-year Middle School teacher in the first week of school? That's what I SHOULD have been thinking, but this was my first year. My "First Week Packet" had all sorts of icebreaker activities planned for the day's first period. Back then, the first period of the day was called "home base". Home Base was designed to help kids as they were getting used to school, and each other again. I selected one of the activities that looked promising. It was mixed in with lame activities, all planned by adults who had clearly lost touch with what it was like to be a middle schooler. The lesson asked students to write three facts about themselves on a piece of paper. The twist was, they were NOT to include their names. An odd choice considering how much time we spend getting kids to do that one first step reliably.

Then, they would fold the piece of paper into an airplane worthy of the Wright Brothers, and throw it. Students were then expected to find, and re-throw three or four paper airplanes. This added to the chaos and increased the random distribution of planes around the classroom. Students would grab the nearest airplane and wait for instructions. Once it was their turn, they would open it up and read the three facts. Then the students in the room would try to guess whose paper it was from the facts. Seems interesting, or at least fun.

Enter Shawn.

Shawn was a quiet, rural kid who would much rather be outdoors than in school. His jeans had dried mud from a short ATV ride he was able to squeeze in before the bus arrived. His oversized brown leather work boots weren't for show but had seen some hard work for a kid his age. Shawn had calluses that would make the shop teacher jealous. He was more grounded and serious than most 7th-grade boys. But, like many of the kids in the class, he knew the same pains as other kids his age. Shawn was a child of divorce. All these things came out in his paper airplane summary. On his paper, in dark, wide pencil marks, were the three facts:

1. I love 4-wheeling.
2. I like to hunt.
3. My dad lives in Virginia.

As Shawn finished his oversimplified life statements, he folded his paper into a plane and waited to "send it". He didn't have to wait long, and chaos ensued. As the chaos died down, I noticed that all the students had retrieved an airplane. Shawn sat in the back of the classroom at one of the octagon black-topped lab tables with an airplane in hand. He was noticeably relaxed as he enjoyed the security of a little extra space. His airplane, however, had landed near the front of the room and was in the hands of none other than Joey.

Enter Joey.

Joey couldn't sit still and rushed through everything. He unfolded the paper airplane and flattened it on the desk with his hand over and over. This was as still as he was capable of waiting.

One by one, kids would read their list and guess whose paper they had. Each successful guess would determine the next person's turn. Then it got to Joey. In true Joey fashion, he looked down and read,

I like to 4-wheel, I love to hunt. And my dad lives in a vagina.

Did he just say, "VAGINA??" In shock, confusion, and mild immaturity, I tried to keep a straight face. I was lacking an important skill at the time. A skill I would master soon as students swapped the word "orgasm" for "organism". The skill of selective ignorance with redirection. But as this was early in my career, I had nothing. That's when clarity struck from the back lab table like lightning on the prairie. Shawn thundered loud and clear, "It's Virginia, Joey. VIR. GIN. YA. My dad lives in VIRGINIA" Mystery solved. Then the bell rang.

Bryan Zevotek is a recovering burned-out teacher. Helping teachers find joy, balance, and sustainability for life and teaching. Author of "Recalculating". Conference speaker, YouTuber, and podcaster. Follow him at @classkicker and check him out at kicksomeclass.com

4 NON-BLONDES
By Joi Chimera

My friend Aimee is a little crazy,? She, Laurie, and Deann love doing funny T-shirts at conferences. At the NYSCATE conference, they made funny shirts and had so much fun. So I told them, "Hey, I'm going to be at FETC by myself. I would love to get in on the fun with you."

They were like, "Okay."

So I sent them money for a T-shirt, and we wore them on the second night we were there. And I thought to myself, *Oh, this is great. I'm so happy to be part of it.* I and assumed everything was over, because I did not contribute to anything other than the T-shirt.

Something to keep in mind, I'm an extroverted introvert. What that means is, I will be happy to talk with people I know, but I'm really not a big fan of people in general, especially if I don't know them. Our last night of the conferenceI was meeting them at dinner, I walked in, and the woman was like, "Oh, you're from New York. Okay, there are some NY people over there. You probably see people that you know."

I quickly did a scan of the room, and because they were all blondes, they pretty much stood out in the room. As I looked around, I was like, *Alright, I don't see any blondes.* I started getting in my head, like, *Where did this lady sit me? Do I have to sit with people that I don't know?* Now I have to gear up and get my game face on to have conversations with strangers.

She's leading me through the room, and I'm walking and still looking around; I don't see them anywhere. As I got a little bit closer, all of a sudden, I looked, and I just started laughing hysterically. The lady had no idea what was going on.

I told the woman, "You don't know this, but those three people are really blonde as I pointed to Aimee, Deann & Laurie. And it still didn't really click. Then Amy pulled her wig off, and the lady and everyone at the table roared with laughter. Apparently, they wanted to dress up as me. I said it's this thing that they do, they always try to beat their craziness. And tonight, apparently, it was a "Night of Joi". So they all had on wigs, black wigs and black glasses. They wore all black because typically I wear all black.because I was wearing the brown jacket, I was out of my "uniform." As the night went on, other people joined in the fun as well. We had a group of bald men who wanted to put the wigs and glasses on and I took photos with them. It will go down as one of the funniest nights ever!

Joi Chimera is a 20+ year educator in New York. She spent most of her career in the Western New York area where she was a classroom teacher and Innovation Support Specialist. She is currently the Assistant Director for Instructional Technology for the City School District of New Rochelle in Westchester County, NY. She is an ISTE and Canvas Certified Educator as well as Google Level I & II certified. She is an avid baseball fan and has visited 21 of the 30 MLB stadiums.

A QUICK LAUGH

One day leaving school a student hugged me goodbye. He took in a deep inhale as they do.

They then smiled and looked at me and said....

"Your shirt smells like old cheese. "

Grade 1 Teacher
Pittsburgh, PA

POTATO FLAKES

By Christine Ravesi-Weinstein

So I'm a first-year teacher, and I'm highly motivated. We all know that starts to dip pretty quickly as the years go by, but that year, I had to teach the students about solutions. They had to know what a solvent was, a solute, and a solution. What dilute means, what a suspension is, right? And so I thought it would be far more engaging to actually mix the solutions with the students in real time, rather than just tell them what they were. I could mix them, and we could talk about what they were seeing. So I spent time at home the night before trying to figure out what materials could make each solution. Obviously, for solute and solvent, we could use sugar or salt; that's easy. But a suspension was harder. You need to find something that, when you put it in water, sinks to the bottom. However, if you introduce a mechanical motion to the solution, like stirring, the material starts to swirl around and will appear to be mixing. However, the second you stop stirring, the material sinks to the bottom again. Basically, it's a snowglobe. But I thought it would be cooler to make a suspension live and present it as chemistry and then say, "Okay, what does this remind you of?" And then maybe a kid would make the connection to a snowglobe, and I'd take one out to show them, create that hook and that relevance.

So I'm at home, I'm living with my mom at the time, and she's enjoying trying to be creative with me. So I'm going through all the stuff in the cabinet, trying to find something that will act as a suspension. I'm trying dry rice; but nothing is working. Anyway, I finally found something: Hungry Jack Potato Flakes. If you put them in cold water, they sink to the bottom, and then if you stir, they mix up, but they don't dissolve; they float around and then they stop. I'm so proud; this is brilliant. I'm a first-year teacher, right, and I'm going to do more than just chalk and talk.

So the suspension is the big act at the end of the demo. We're going to make the boring solutions first, right, and then build up to this suspension.

We get to the suspension demo and I start making it: I pour the potato flakes into the water, I start stirring it up, and the kids are like, "Oh, wow!" I stop stirring and the flakes immediately sink back to the bottom of the beaker.

I asked the class, "So what do you think this is?" Now we get to play the guessing game; that whole need to know, right? And so kids are like, "Is it rice?"

"No, it's not rice."

Someone eventually says, "Are those potato flakes?"

And I'm like, "Yes! They're potato flakes! Isn't that amazing?!"

And they're like, "Yeah, that's so cool!"

"So what does this remind you of?" I asked.

And as planned, a student is like, "It reminds me of a snow globe."

"Yes!" I say so proud that the demo worked. So I take out a snow globe, and shake it up, then put it down, and it settles. And so this kid who was a really sweet kid and I liked her a lot, but maybe she wasn't the brightest kid. She was really gullible and not super academic or into school opens her eyes wide and drops her jaw; she's in the midst of one of those moments you dream of as a teacher: a light bulb moment.

So in front of the whole class, she goes, "Oh, my God!"

And I pause and say, "Yeah?"

And she yells out, "*SO THAT'S WHAT'S IN A SNOWGLOBE!*"

So that's what I accomplished. I got this girl to believe that Hungry Jack Potato Flakes were what was in a snowglobe. So I fell miserably with her to understand.

I leave that day, and I go home. My mom can't wait to hear how it went. "So how did it go?" she asks as soon as I walk through the door.

"Well," I start, "one girl took away that Hungry Jack Potato Flakes and water are what's in a snowglobe. So, well, I think. It went well."

FIELD TRIPS...REALLY

By Laurie Guyon

Our 6th-grade team would take our students into the Adirondacks for outdoor education. We would sleep in basic cabins, eat in a dining hall and explore the great outdoors for three days.

One year, we had a boy who didn't pack the right hiking clothes. He ended up in thick jeans, wool socks, and dress shoes. We encouraged him to change before heading out, but he said he had nothing else to wear. So off he went hiking the mountain. About halfway up the mountain, we stopped for a quick snack of apple slices. He was already struggling, but we thought the stop would help him and encouraged him to adjust his socks and do what he could to get comfortable. Little did we know that the socks were not the issue. As we started again, he would stop every two minutes and adjust himself. As we encouraged him to keep climbing, he became increasingly distressed. He was in so much pain when he reached the top. We asked him what was hurting. He finally admitted that he had severe chaffing in "some parts of his body" that he didn't want to discuss. There was nothing we could do to help him! As we headed down the mountain, we realized that this chafing was so bad he could barely walk. What should have been a 3-hour hike turned into a 6-hour one as he crawled down the mountain.

Our 6th-grade team would take our students into the Adirondacks for outdoor education. We would sleep in basic cabins, eat in a dining hall and explore the great outdoors for three days.

Another year we had one boy who swore he had nothing besides the clothes on his back. He swore we lost his bag or left it at school when we arrived at the camp. We gave him some toiletries and whatever we could, but he basically wore the same clothes all three days. When we got back to the school, and his parents came to pick him up, they grabbed a bag from the pile. We told the parents that he said he had no clothes. The bag they had claimed had sat under a tree at the camp for three days because no one had claimed it. It turns out his parents had packed for him, and loaded the bag on the bus, so he had no idea it was his bag! The lesson learned here was that 6th graders should be involved in the packing!

To close this book, I wanted the last story to be about joy and living, a message of support, care, and joy no matter the classroom or country. We are one educational community driven to be the best for kids and each other.

LEARNING AND LAUGHING SIDE-BY-SIDE

By Eugenia Tamez

Being invited to share a moment of happiness and laughter, I wanted to add to the original list of #SameHereGlobal statements listed in the introduction with a proactive lens to the work we collectively do as educators:

- If you work with students and school communities who don't have access to technology and other resources but are still always curious and eager to learn, **same here**.
- If you experience how learning side-by-side with students, colleagues, and the entire school community positively changes the school culture, **same here**.
- If you create moments where students can actively solve problems and create solutions as a way to create positive ripples of change, **same here**.
- If you design learning experiences for an entire school community to learn *with* students, **same here**.

- If you intentionally focus on bringing more laughter and joy back into your classroom and school community, **same here**.

My work involves inviting Latin American school communities to learn and practice using technology for good. I've noticed over the years that no matter where you live, what resources are available to you, the language(s) you speak, or how young or old you are – we are better and stronger together. Even if students don't have access to tech at school, cell phones, and internet cafes are available to check social media, play video games or just surf the internet.

One memory full of laughter was when I was working with a school community in Oaxaca, a beautiful city in southern Mexico where the population is extremely poor. The scholar level is almost the lowest in the country, but on the other hand, people are kind, happy, and cheerful. Despite access to technology at the school, we created groups based on social media platforms. For example, "I'm a social media platform that is used especially by grownups," or "I'm a really special platform with filters,"..... and so on...and so on. Everyone was laughing and learning about the differences and similarities between platforms. In the end, each team had to present to the other teams everything they learned about the social media platform they represented and without even knowing this was a teachable moment, the students learned more information about digital citizenship and how to create safe spaces for themselves and others, how to solve real problems, and how to become a force for good both on and offline.

What made this particular memory special for me? It was a moment in time when we modeled learning side-by-side and learning alongside the students. It is a reminder that we must create more moments like this where students have fun learning, and smiles and laughter support curiosity.

@etamez
DigCit and Educational
Technology consultant

FINAL THOUGHTS

In this journey through fun and sometimes unbelievable stories, we shared giggles and highlighted the importance of laughter in education. Also, I hope you realize all that teachers do every day, all day. I believe laughter is a transformative force that can shape our students' minds and hearts. Laughter, often considered a simple pleasure, is a profound tool that can unlock the doors to effective and joyful learning. Combined with the #SameHereGlobal message, it shows in this big world, we are all connected.

Sure, this laughter was more about stories and a moment in time. But I have seen that by infusing our classrooms with laughter, we create an optimal environment for students to absorb knowledge, retain information, and truly enjoy the process of learning. Yes, these stories were funny for what was said or done, but infusing laughter into schools is an important part of the educational journey.

Beyond the academic benefits, I have seen how laughter fosters strong bonds between educators and students. When laughter fills the classroom, it breaks down barriers and establishes an atmosphere of trust and camaraderie. Students feel comfortable expressing themselves, taking risks, and embracing failure as part of the learning process.

It is not about neglecting academic rigor, but rather, it is about enhancing it with the magic of laughter. It is about finding creative ways to incorporate humor into lesson plans, encouraging playful interactions, and fostering an atmosphere where laughter is tolerated and celebrated.

The responsibility lies with us to create learning environments that nurture the curiosity and joy inherent in every child. We must challenge outdated practices that stifle creativity and replace them with innovative approaches that encourage laughter, critical thinking, and a love for learning.

Let us empower our teachers to embrace humor as a powerful teaching tool and support them in creating a positive and uplifting classroom culture. As parents, let us value the significance of laughter in our children's lives and instill in them a sense of wonder and excitement about learning.

As we move forward, let us embark on a laughter revolution in education, where the stifling burden of stress is replaced with the lightness of joy, where the thrill of exploration overshadows the fear of failure, and where the flames of laughter kindle the love for learning.

ABOUT DR. MATTHEW X. JOSEPH

Dr. Matthew X. Joseph has been a school and district leader in many capacities in public education over his 28 years in the field. Experiences such as Executive Director of Teaching and Learning, the Director of Curriculum and Instruction, Director of Digital Learning and Innovation, elementary school principal, classroom teacher, and district professional

development specialist have provided Matt incredible insights on how to best support teaching and learning and led to nationally published articles and opportunities to speak at multiple state and national events. His master's degree is in special education and his Ed.D. in Educational Leadership from Boston College. He is the author of Stronger Together: The Power of Connections Within a School Community, Power Of Connections: Connecting Educators, Cultivating Professional Learning Networks, & Redefining Educator Collaboration, and co-author of Modern Mentor, Reimagining Mentorship in Education and Disrupt the Status Quo.

Matt is the CEO of X-Factor EDU. X-Factor EDU started in 2016 after he finished his Ed.D in educational leadership from Boston College. He began his journey to supporting educators and districts. X-Factor EDU is a full-service professional development organization with educators from multiple countries and backgrounds. In addition to publishing the voice of amazing educators, we provide leadership coaching, district consulting and workshops, and keynotes around many educational topics.

Matt is the president of MASCD (The Massachusetts chapter of ASCD) and recognized in 2021 as one of 10 national leaders on the rise.

To learn more about Matt or book him for a visit to your school, district, or event visit https://mxjedu.net

ABOUT THE EDITORS

I am deeply grateful for the amazing journey we have undertaken together in bringing this project to fruition. To all my esteemed collaborators, thank you from the bottom of my heart for your unwavering dedication, creativity, and sharing of your stories. Each of you brought unique skills and perspectives to the table, enriching this book beyond my expectations. Together, we have proven that the power of collaboration knows no bounds, and I am profoundly honored to have shared this journey with such an incredible group of individuals. Thank you for your unyielding belief in this project and for being the true creators of its success. Besides stories, we have had three individual help organize this work and edit when needed.

Internationally recognized as a digital citizenship expert, **Dr. Marialice B.F.X. Curran** is an educator, consultant, and speaker who is the global connector behind the Digital Citizenship Institute. Committed to Human-Centered Design, Dr. Curran is a school community architect who leads by hand, heart, and

mind as she models how to make a positive impact in local, global, and digital communities. She has served as an associate professor, and middle school teacher and principal. As a connected educator, her intergenerational work with school communities around the world has created positive and powerful shifts in how we engage and learn at school, home, play, and work.

Sarah Laliberte has worked as a writer and editor in the publishing industry for over 18 years. She brings a passion for words to her writing and editing in order to create clear and engaging content. Sarah enjoys helping other writers bring their writing into focus, and she aims to share information and ideas in a way that tickles readers' brains. Sarah is an alumni of the North Carolina School of Science and Mathematics and the University of North Carolina at Chapel Hill. She currently lives in the Blue Ridge Mountains of North Carolina.

Christine Ravesi-Weinstein currently serves as a high school Assistant Principal in Massachusetts, USA and previously worked as a high school science department chair for four years and classroom teacher for 15. Diagnosed with anxiety and depression at 23, Christine began her journey towards mental wellness. She began a non-profit organization in June of 2017 aimed at removing the stigma of mental illness and promoting physical activity as a means to cope with anxiety.

As an avid writer and educator, Christine became passionate about bridging the two with her advocacy for mental health.Christine has presented at numerous national conferences and has provided professional development for educators in various districts. Follow her work on Twitter @RavesiWeinstein and on YouTube at http://bit.ly/TheRunnersHigh. For more information about Christine, please visit her website at www.ravesiweinstein.com

View our services, catalog of books, and meet our team of authors at https://xfactoredu.org.

Our team of educators are using their voice, journey, experiences, and practices to be the catalyst for change in education.

Visit: https://xfactoredu.org

LEADERSHIP SERIES

KID COLLECTION

Made in the USA
Columbia, SC
16 June 2024

36770178R00065